Max It Out!

Discover how $25 a month can unlock
a lifetime of financial security.

Second Edition

BRENDA CAROLINA PAZ

Library of Congress Cataloging-in-Publication Data

Brenda Carolina Paz,
Max It Out! Discover how $25 a month can unlock a lifetime of financial security.
Edited by: Clara Abigail
Published by: Giselle Salazar Photography

Library of Congress Control Number: 2012902336

ISBN: 979-8-9919211-2-1

Printed in the United States of America

Note: This book is intended only as an informative guide for those wishing to know about investing. Readers are advised to consult a professional Financial Advisor before making any financial decisions. The reader assumes all responsibility for the consequences of any actions taken based on the information presented in this book. The information in this book is based on the author's research and experience. Every attempt has been made to ensure that the information is accurate; however, the author cannot accept liability for any errors that may exist. The facts and theories on investing and finances are subject to interpretation, and the conclusions and recommendations presented here may not agree with other interpretations.

Scan the QR code to download the **"Fund Tracking Sheet" for FREE!**

Take control of your investments with *My Fund Tracking Sheet*, a simple yet powerful tool to manage and track all your investments in one place.

Join the Movement

Scan the QR code below to access the **Feminine Finance Mastery Community**— where ambitious women learn to invest with confidence, build wealth, and live in abundance.

REVIEWS FOR MAX IT OUT!

"This book is an easy read for someone who has never invested a dollar in their life. It paints a vivid picture of her investment and personal journey, and her personal story is inspiring. This book is a perfect gift for anyone. However, it benefits anyone starting their career out of school or entering the military." - Dr. Ainsley A. Reynolds

"Brenda, this book is sooo good!! I read the whole book in one night. I couldn't put it down. I looooved the tips in the story line. Such a great idea. Honestly it's perfect for me too cause I'm a newbie and have been wanting to get into investing but I'm like what are all these terms lol. It's very easy to read and understand and honestly makes me feel so much better in getting started as a newbie. Love all the examples too. Thank you so much for writing this book. I know it will help soooo many people. Can't wait to max it out with you ♡ " - Mazzy

"Max It Out stands out for its authenticity, storytelling, and distilled wisdom. The author shares real-life stories and lessons in a way that's both engaging and practical. One of my favorite features is that key points are easy to reference, as each chapter recaps the lessons at the end. No matter where you are in your financial journey, the advice is precise and

accessible. If you're looking for engaging storytelling paired with valuable insights, I highly recommend this book." - Anonymous.

"This book is a must buy. It had my whole interest from beginning to the end. I read the whole book. Brenda C. Hall shares all her learning experiences and was determined to succeed. I don't want to write too much because you'll have to read the book for yourself. Love how real she was in the book. Get it you won't regret it. I loved and enjoyed it. Going to re-read it again. Thank you for writing such an amazing book." - AJ

CONTENTS

FOREWORD

The year was 1993. I had the pleasure of working for the New Brunswick Police Department and running a community center that graced me with the opportunity to work with young minds in the town I was born in. This assignment with the New Brunswick Police Department fed my hunger for working with young people. Shortly after my assignment, I met this quiet, introverted, beautiful young girl, recently arriving here from Honduras. Though she didn't have a complete grasp of the culture or language, she appeared eager to learn and fit in. Though I loved many kids who crossed my path at my assignment, I was immediately drawn to Brenda Paz.

Brenda would spend countless hours in my office during and after school. She always excelled through every challenge that was given to her, eager to learn attitude. Roosevelt School was a kindergarten through eighth-grade institution, so our time together, like with all students, would be short-lived. Brenda went to New Brunswick High, and life went on.

Most kids that came through the programs we hosted grew up and grew on. I would rarely ever interact with them again. Social media wasn't widely available so there was no way to get insight on anyone's life without having real conversations with them.

As my career excelled, I had the opportunity to attend the Police Academy and start my career in law enforcement as a sworn officer. A big hurdle for me was the military cadence, the regiment, the understanding of drills, and marching. I was very close to being kicked out of the academy through my failures.

My biggest challenge? "About-face!" My drill sergeant gave me one week to figure it out or I was done, and my dreams of becoming a sworn officer would diminish. I went back to Roosevelt School and contemplated my future.

A petite soldier outfitted in a military dress uniform approached my office displaying their best military battalion march. It was Brenda Paz, now a ROTC officer at the high school's program. She was eager to tell me all about her uniform and what it represented as an ROTC candidate. I told Brenda of my difficulties in the academy, and she said she could teach me in seconds. Though the interaction may seem minimal, it has stuck with me for many years to follow. It allowed me to continue my career.

Brenda and I had several more occasions when we crossed paths, and I always reflected upon that time she helped me get through the academy. Life continued, and Brenda moved on. Full-time military, relationships, and the birth of her daughter. We continued to stay connected. It is easy to revel in her many successes and feel that you may have had some small part in it happening, but the truth is being around Brenda has helped me grow. I look forward to all the future chapters that haven't been written.

When you read a book, whether self-help or autobiographical, you rarely share encounters with the author. Brenda Paz is the blueprint for the proverbial "American Dream." A young girl whose family migrated from a foreign country, to a "roll up your sleeves" grass-rooted success story. Brenda has put in the labor to become successful. When she decided to write a book, I could not think of anyone better to share their story. I've been blessed to witness the struggle and share in her riches.

 Follow the path that she has blazed in an opportunity to make your life more fulfilling and financially stable. I hope you enjoy the book as much as I enjoyed the unedited pre-copy.

Lamont Bowling
CEO of Atlantic City Fashion Week

PREFACE

Throughout my investing journey, I've read many books on personal finance, trading stocks, and long-term investing. I've also taken personal financial courses, but most importantly, I have the personal experience of making so many mistakes in the past twenty-three years of investing. One huge mistake was that of having trusted the Certified Financial Advisor at my bank, who just told me not to put all of my eggs in one basket and he chose where to put my hard-earned money. Because, let's face it, if you're like me, I came from nothing. I didn't make much money either when I joined the military in 2000. When I checked my earnings record history on the social security website, I made $11,244 in the year 2000 and $15,622 the next year, and it increased approximately three thousand per year after that.

Regardless of the minimal salary, I still invested. Unfortunately, I trusted that these financial advisors would guide me or perhaps teach me how to invest, but I was caught in the "investing world" with the financial words that seemed like they were coming from another planet. Mutual fund what? Allocation who? Index que? Yeah, that's too much for *this*

Latina who learned English as a second language, I thought to myself.

I experienced this thing called "imposter syndrome." Who the hell am I to understand investing? I've already achieved what none of my family members have achieved. So I trusted that my money was being invested to make me win big. LMAO! Yeah, okay, I found out the hard way, and I share those lessons as you read this book.

One day during a gratitude meditation, the idea of writing this book popped into my head. I mean, friends and family ask me about investing, so I thought, Why not put it in a book so that I can share my story with more people on how I started my investing journey? So here I am writing this book at any chance I get, mostly at night, 11 p.m. to be exact because for whatever reason my focus is better at night. I hope that you find this book useful and that you implement the tips and lessons I've included.

LIST OF DEFINED TERMS FOR BEGINNER INVESTORS

Term	Definition	Analogy
Stock	A stock represents partial ownership in a company and entitles the holder to a share of its profits.	Owning a stock is like having a slice of a cake: if the cake grows, your slice grows too.
Bond	A bond is a loan an investor gives to an entity (government or company) in exchange for regular interest payments.	Buying a bond is like lending money to a friend and receiving interest until they repay you.
ETF (Exchange-Traded Fund)	An investment fund traded on an exchange that holds a mix of assets like stocks or bonds.	It's like a mixed fruit basket: instead of buying just apples, you buy a variety of fruits.
Mutual Fund	A fund that pools money from many investors to purchase a diversified portfolio of assets.	Like a shared savings pool where everyone contributes and benefits based on their input.

List of Defined Terms for Beginner Investors

Term	Definition	Analogy
Index Fund	A mutual fund or ETF that mirrors a market index like the S&P 500.	Like a box of assorted chocolates that exactly matches a store's selection.
Dividend	A payment a company makes to shareholders from its profits.	Like getting a bonus tip for owning a part of the business.
Capital Gain	The profit made from selling an asset at a higher price than it was bought.	Like buying a cheap house, fixing it up, and selling it at a higher price.
Expense Ratio	The percentage of a fund's assets used to cover operational costs.	Like paying a small management fee for someone to tend your garden.
401(k)	A retirement savings plan sponsored by an employer with tax benefits.	Like a special piggy bank where your employer also adds money.
Roth IRA	An individual retirement account where contributions are made with after-tax money and withdrawals are tax-free.	Like paying for a feast in advance and enjoying the meal for free later.

Term	Definition	Analogy
Asset Allocation	The strategy of spreading investments across different asset types to manage risk.	Like balancing a diet with various foods to stay healthy.
Risk Tolerance	An investor's ability to handle ups and downs in investment value.	Like choosing between a wild roller coaster or a gentler ride.
Compound Interest	Interest calculated on both the initial principal and the previously accumulated interest.	Like a snowball rolling downhill, growing bigger over time.
Liquidity	How easily an asset can be converted to cash without losing value.	Like having cash versus owning a house: cash is easy to use, selling a house takes time.

INTRODUCTION

Max it out? When you picked up this book, I bet you were thinking, "What does it mean to max it out? Max out my credit card? What am I maxing out? My 401k? How can I max out my 401k when I don't make that much?"

Max It Out is not about maxing out credit cards. It's not about initially maxing out your investments. It's about you starting your investing journey with as little as twenty-five dollars a month and eventually maxing out your contributions if your salary permits. Most importantly, it's to Max It Out in life to what your current financial situation allows. If you can only afford twenty-five dollars a month, then you've Maxed It Out. If you can invest double or triple, then you've Maxed It Out as well. See the point here is that in the investment world, you have to *start*, and the sooner the better.

I started investing in my early twenties when I was in the Navy making $11,244 per year. I started investing with a measly twenty-five bucks a month! Yes, sir or ma'am, twenty-five dollars! Unfortunately, I invested blindly, not knowing what the heck I was doing. I just called my bank and asked them to automatically take those twenty-five bucks out of my bank account and put them into a Roth IRA. Knowing what I know now, I should have checked where that money was going well, it was also my ignorance and limiting belief that I could never learn how to invest.

If you don't already know the steps of investing in a Roth IRA, well I'm about to tell you. First, you open a Roth IRA account. Next, you get your bank to automatically fund the IRA. But here's the kicker: when it gets funded, it goes into those Core accounts, which is essentially a savings account, so the money just sits there if *you* don't figure out where to invest it. Once you know which funds you want to invest in, then you can have your brokerage firm—Fidelity or Vanguard, for example—make that trade (buy) it for you. Or, if you're computer savvy, you can do this yourself. This is a major lesson learned for me. I have no idea where my bank's financial advisor invested my money, and most likely it was a high-fees mutual fund. I don't want this to happen to you, so read on.

CHAPTER 1

Humble Beginnings

Who's Brenda? Oh man, I think it will take an autobiography to tell you all about me. In the meantime, let me tell you a little bit about where I come from and how I got to this point in my investment journey. I was born in Honduras, in a very small, dirt-poor town. Yes, dirt-poor. My grandmother owned a house made of cinder blocks and had a tin roof—okay, I guess we had a roof over our heads, right? That was a good come up for my grandmother compared to where my mom and I grew up, we had cardboard for insulation.

Anyways, that roof would make so much noise when it rained. It was annoying at first, but then somehow you end up getting used to it, and it becomes sort of like white noise to your ears. In this one-bedroom house lived seven people. The bedroom was shared by my grandmother, my grandmother's adopted daughter, my mom, my baby sister, and me. The living room was huge, so my uncles slept there on a "petate," a Spanish word for a sleeping mat made of the woven fibers of a palm tree. You're practically sleeping on the hard floor and will wake up with lower back or shoulder pain.

My mother used to work long hours at a wood factory, sanding and varnishing wooden dinner table legs. I remember tasting her food, and it smelled and tasted like varnish. Any kind of meat was a luxury, so meals were "margarita" cookies and coffee in the mornings. Lunch consisted of egg, beans, and tortillas. Sometimes we'd have sour cream. Everything depended on who brought in some money, and most of the time it was my mother who brought it to feed a family of seven. To be honest, all I remember is my uncles being drunk all the time and causing chaos and stealing from us. My mom would put a lock on our dresser so that they wouldn't steal our clothes to sell them for weed and alcohol.

So, you see, I don't come from money. I come from humble beginnings. I was blessed to have had the opportunity to migrate to the United States at a very early age, but again, my living conditions weren't optimal here either. Growing up I think I had like seven or eight addresses. We moved around so much; they could literally label us as nomads. We lived all over New Brunswick, NJ. Throop Avenue, Remsen, Bayard St, Railroad Ave., I have more addresses, but you get the point.

I never had my own room. We usually lived in a room in the attic, a basement apartment that flooded every time we had a huge rainstorm, near a railroad. I mean, you could have easily high-fived the passengers, that's how close we lived next to it, and my room was in a food pantry closet. Imagine being fifteen years old, and your room is next to the kitchen? Thinking about it, that was so embarrassing, but somehow, I was grateful and super happy with my pantry room. I never complained to my mother nor told her how I felt about it.

Now living in the U.S., eleven-year-old Brenda would dream of owning a house and working in an office like those people in the movies. I think it was a scene from *Look Who's Talking* where I saw women dressed in suits and briefcases and I thought, *I'm going to be like that woman one day. I'm smart enough.* At that age, I couldn't understand why my mother and stepdad didn't want that kind of life or at least, I never heard them talking about it. I thought, *How hard could that be? What do I need to do to achieve this?*

I remember a classmate who was from Mexico. Her mother and father owned a Mexican restaurant. They had it all, and all I could do was dream that one day I could live like they lived. Her father would take me to school in his big Ford pickup and my friend would feed me some Mexican fried quesadillas for breakfasts. They were nice to me. I could just imagine how nice their home might have been. I didn't know how or when, but I knew I wanted more than how I was living.

Fast forward to 2023, I now know the power of investing. I've invested in educating myself, be it taking courses, reading books, listening to Audibles, etc. Along the journey, I've made so many mistakes, many due to lack of education. So, with this book I'm hoping to inspire you to take control of your money and help overcome your fears of investing. I'll share my lessons and strategies that I've learned over these twenty-three years that have allowed me to grow my retirement portfolio to over *three hundred fifty thousand dollars*. Oh, how I wish I knew then what I know now because I would probably be a millionaire by now! My strategy would have been to Max It Out, baby!

CHAPTER 2

Mr. Williams

In September 2000, I started my freshmen year of college at Kean University. I was an NJ Scholar, had a scholarship from Robert Wood Johnson, but it wasn't enough to get me through all four years of school. I owned a FORD (Fix or Repair Daily), as kids in the neighborhood used to joke around anytime someone would say they owned a Ford. (My bad, Ford, I ironically own some of your stocks hehehe). It was a Ford Tempo, to be specific. Man, that car used to break down on me so much.

I was working at the school library to get a discount on books, and worked at Rainforest Café as well. I really hated working there. I got a one-dollar tip because my food was taken to another table and the big party was angry. Yeah, I quit that place. I ended up working at the local hospital near my mom's house as a Patient Escort which involved transporting patients all over the hospital to get x-rays or scans. I really didn't like that job title; people would look at me funny when I used to say I was a Patient Escort.

Mr. Williams

I think I worked every job in the book to make ends meet. I've always been a workaholic trying to fulfill that childhood dream. I started working at age fifteen, making $592 that year, and have had a job ever since. I was able to get my earnings record from the Social Security website, see below from 1995 to 2006.

2006	$19,577
2005	$24,728
2004	$23,317
2003	$20,426
2002	$17,738
2001	$15,622
2000	$11,244
1999	$6,094
1998	$7,628
1997	$4,259
1996	$4,116
1995	$592

One day, trying to go home for the weekend since I lived in the dorm at Kean University my freshman year, my Ford Tempo broke down on me. I took it to a local auto shop, and they told me it was like two hundred bucks to fix an electrical issue they found. At that point, I owed the bank money—

seriously, my account had a negative number on it. As I walked over to pick up my car, I cried so hard on the side of the road. I sobbed as I walked, and I looked up at the sky and, not caring if anyone saw me, I yelled to God, "Please God, give me a sign. What can I do? I can't afford to go to school. Please help me. Give me a sign."

I had no one to guide me, to sit me down and lay out any options on how to fund my school. Thinking about it now, I'm not sure why I didn't go speak to my counselor? Perhaps it was because people back then were ruthless. There were very few people who cared and would want to help you. At least, that was my personal experience. Students have so much information nowadays. It's so accessible. You can go to "YouTube University" to learn more about funding your education. We didn't have social media back then.

When I got home that same afternoon after picking my car up and being indebted to First Union Bank, I received a call from a long-time friend whom I hadn't heard from in over a year. His name is Richard. He was a Navy recruiter who tried to recruit me in my senior year of high school, but I told him that I was a college girl. Hahaha, never say never, right? Like my grandmother used to say, "Don't spit up because the spit will come right down on your face." It sounds better in Spanish, but you get the point.

Over the phone, I screamed, "Richard! You're the answer to my prayers! I want to join the Navy."

He was like, "Oh no, you're a college girl, remember? I don't want you to hate me if you don't like it."

"You don't understand," I said. "I have no money for school, so I have to join the Navy."

He agreed to help, but he assigned me to another recruiter. Joining the Navy wasn't easy for me; I had to lose weight. I had already taken the ASFAV and scored decently, but because I'm five-foot-two, I didn't meet the height to weight requirements, so there was another hurdle I had to cross. So, I bought a bottle of xenadrine and back then, it had ephedra. Holy smokes! I ran for two months, and I swear I could have died from cardiac arrest. That ephedra was no joke. I remember coming back from a long run, and my face was beet-red, heart pounding like I was having a frigging panic attack, and I just fell onto the floor to catch my breath. The use of ephedra was banned in 2004 because it caused heart attacks, seizures, strokes, and sudden death. Thank God I stopped using that supplement.

So, I dropped out of college, lost over twenty pounds, and off to the Navy I went. At MEPS, the medical processing place, they were trying to make me take a job as a religious professional. I looked at them like they were crazy. I told them no and took my friend Richard's advice to go aviation, so they offered me a job handling bombs. I said, "Oh, hells no, I don't want to touch bombs or electricity." So, I picked an aircraft mechanic.

I wasn't afraid at all going into bootcamp. I think it was my determination and drive to get myself into college. Richard had instructed me that if my goal was to go to college, then stay in aviation, preferably on P-3 Orion—those planes don't land on the ship—so my probability of going to school while in the Navy was a lot higher than being on the ship. But here's the kicker: in A-school for aviation mechanics, in order to be able to pick your duty station, you have to be in the top three. So I studied my butt off, day and night. Flashcards were my best friends. I ended up being in second place, so I picked P-3 in Jacksonville, Florida.

At my first duty station in Jax, I started working as First Lieutenant. This is basically a glorified name for doing janitorial duties for up to a year or so. The duties I performed were stripping and waxing floors, cleaning the bathrooms and office spaces. We used to joke around, "I didn't sign up to clean toilets."

Then I remember someone saying, "The shitters can't clean themselves. Somebody's gotta do it." So true and well, that was the enlistment process for new airmen. That was where I met Petty Officer First Class, Williams. He is a kind-hearted man. He cared so much for the well-being of all the new airmen. One day, we were all sitting around during the break, and he said, "Hey, do you guys know what a Roth IRA is?"

Of course, I'm going to listen attentively because I had that insatiable hunger to one day be financially stable.

Mr. Williams

"Well it's this new savings account for retirement," he went on, "and you put your money there, and it's tax-free when you take it out by age fifty-nine and a half."

He planted that seed in my head, and of course I had to do something about it. At the time we didn't have Google but I did some research, and something told me to start with twenty-five dollars a month. That's three hundred dollars a year and in the year 2000, the max contribution limit was two thousand dollars.

By the way, Mr. Williams and I are still friends twenty-two years later, and we spoke about how he planted the seed for me to start investing and to my surprise, he never invested in a Roth IRA. That took me aback because I thought that he had invested since he told us about it. I told him everything I'd learned until that phone call. He's always been extremely supportive, and I appreciate him till this day.

Lesson #1: If you're in your twenties and your salary permits, you should invest the max Roth IRA contribution limit. Do it! If your salary doesn't allow you to max out, then invest in what you're comfortable with. You've heard "Pay yourself first!" Yes, love yourself, pay yourself. You'll be on the path to wealth in the long run. If I could go back, I would have done this. If you're older than thirty, it's not too late. This tip applies to you as well.

I tell anyone I mentor to take ten percent from your salary for your savings and investments. So, let's say you make forty thousand dollars a year. Calculate ten percent of that. So, four thousand dollars can be divided into savings, Roth IRA, 401k buckets. How much in each depends on how much savings you currently have and how much matching your employer gives you for your 401k. You'll have to figure those amounts to fit your needs.

My mom and stepfather wanted to move to Florida to see if they would like it, so I was able to live off-base and rented a three-bedroom apartment so they could live with me while they found jobs and got their own place. Military pay, with BAH (rent money), was not a lot and one day I noticed that I couldn't make ends meet. I wanted to help my family, but renting that apartment had me living paycheck to paycheck. Every time the rent came, I was breaking a sweat because I didn't have enough, so I decided to work part-time at the mall.

I worked at a dollar store as a closing supervisor. I met a man there who also gave me a gig being the Easter Bunny for extra cash, so I managed to pay the rent and other bills. What a relief. I thought to myself, *I never want to be in this situation again*, so it occurred to me to set a goal to never go below a thousand dollars in my checking account. And so I did. I've always had this drive and desire, that thing nowadays they call "manifestation." I call it "setting goals and sticking to them in order to achieve them." So, I began to save money and managed to get to a thousand dollars, and any time my account would go below that by one dollar, I immediately would stop spending until it was back up. I still do this 'till this day. It feels so good to know that you don't have to worry about ever living paycheck to paycheck again.

> *Lesson #2: If you can relate, then I challenge you to commit to saving at least a thousand dollars in your checking and never go below that amount. Trust me, it works! It's like your subconscious won't allow you to go below it. You must be consistent and commit to this. Whatever you do, do not touch that money. It's your emergency stash. Now, if you can commit to saving more, do it. I started with one thousand, then five thousand and increased as needed.*

So, during my time at this duty station, I set and achieved the following goals: made Petty Officer Second Class within two years, became a U.S citizen, and started taking one college class at a time. I achieved all three goals, and it was time for my next duty station in Hawaii.

CHAPTER 3

Focused

Although my duty station was in Kaneohe Bay, Hawaii, I had to deploy for six months to Misawa, Japan. Japan was beautiful, and because I had the scarcity mindset, I didn't want to spend any money. I really didn't get to enjoy much of the beautiful country and culture. To top it off, we were also restricted due to the 9/11 events which occurred in 2001. At this duty station, I asked for permission to enroll in school and began using the Navy's tuition assistance to take one college class at a time. That was my main goal when I joined the Navy, so my focus and energy were on that goal.

Our work schedule was twelve on, twelve off. On my off time, I would walk in the freezing cold bundled up in my parka and go over the high inches of white snow to the elementary school on the base where my classes were held. While going to school, I never thought about my investments because my Roth was getting automatically funded. At that point, I think I had increased it to fifty bucks a month since I made rank—

in other words, got promoted. When I opened the account, I just set it to automatically deduct and never looked back. I just let it be.

> *Lesson #3: Set it to automatically deduct from your bank account. I'm sure you've heard the phrase before: "Set it and forget it!" That's right! Do the same with your Roth and/or 401k. You don't have to be a genius to do this. If you're not technical, ask a friend or family member to help you. Go to YouTube University so there is no excuse for you to say that you can't do it. Now go automate your investments.*

I remember that I would always keep looking at my investments to see how they were doing. I kept thinking, *What if I die? What's going to happen to my money? I'm not going to enjoy it; others will. What if the stock market crashes?* Believe me, I had those anxieties, but some fears are typically from lack of knowledge, and others stem from having some friends who would say things to me like, "Oh, why do you want to save so much? We're going to die one day, and you're going to leave all of that money there and never enjoy it?" Those words will subconsciously mess with your mind, and at one point I wanted to take my money out, which brings me to Lesson #4.

Lesson #4: First, acquire as much knowledge as possible so that you have a better understanding of what you're getting into. Second, ignore the naysayers. If your friends aren't supporting your goals, drop them. I know it sounds mean, but like Les Brown says, "If you hang out with nine broke people, you'll become number ten!" Um, yes, this is true. So, be mindful of whom you tell your goals and aspirations to—not everyone is clapping for you. Surround yourself with like-minded people that support your goals and vision.

It was now summer of '03, and we're back in Hawaii. Oh, the beautiful island of Oahu where it is sunny, with perfect weather, and just lovely views of mountains and flowers and beautiful aquamarine-colored beaches, but I never got to enjoy it. I lived in Hawaii for two and a half years and thinking about it now, other than Oahu, the other Island I got to visit was Maui for my 23rd birthday but none of the other islands. I never did *anything* fun or adventurous during my time there. I really thought I couldn't afford it, plus I had immediately enrolled in classes at Hawaii Pacific University and kept my focus on my purpose, which was to earn that degree. One day I decided I would increase my Roth IRA contribution to a hundred dollars a month. I must have been looking at my account and saw the growth, so I thought to myself, *Going forward, every year that I get a raise, I'm going to increase the amount of investment I make to this account.*

> *Lesson #5: Do this every time you get a raise. Increase it by five, ten, fifteen dollars a month until you get to the amount you're comfortable with. Every little increase helps get you closer to your goal. Eventually, you'll want to max that Roth or 401k or whatever investment account you have. Yearly contribution limits vary depending on the current year so make sure you check what they are for the Roth IRA and 401k.*

This same year, I started dating someone I worked with. He was a Navy Aircrew man. I had met him back in 2000 in Florida, but we began our friendship/relationship in Hawaii. We would always talk at work anytime we would cross paths. I was an aircraft mechanic so we only saw each other when he or I were on duty. I was so excited that he was around my age and was the same rank as me, and we hit it off. He asked me to be his girlfriend at McDonalds on base. Oh, how romantic, huh? It was cute in my twenties though.

A couple of months later, it was time to deploy again. I couldn't go and had to stay back because I had developed some abnormal blood vessels in my right eye which caused it to leak, similar to wet macular degeneration but not age-related. This happened out of the blue, and I needed eye injections and a laser treatment. To my surprise, I was also pregnant. My boyfriend left on deployment, and I stayed back.

, I would waddle to my classes for the next nine months. One day while driving to class, I grabbed some Burger King. As I got close to the main gate of the base, I rolled my window down, and I got a whiff of the ocean, a strong, putrid smell of marine life. I wanted to pull over to the side of the road to puke. I held it together, got to class, put my bookbag on the desk, and ran to the bathroom to throw up all the Burger King. Yeah, that's what I did in school and work during my pregnancy. Now that I had a little human being in my womb, I was even *more* determined to finish that degree. I went full force!

February 18, 2005, I gave birth to my princess. That was one of the happiest and scariest days of my life. Yes, scary too because I was a new mom, and a single mother, to make it even better—yeah, I said *better*—since it didn't work out with her dad.

I had my final presentation for my marketing class due the week after giving birth to my daughter. I went to class, feet and face all swollen, and gave my presentation. Hey, a woman's gotta do what a woman's gotta do. I ended up walking at my graduation in June of '05 with my Associate in Marketing with honors. That Associate took me five years to earn. Since military pay was not that much according to government guidelines, I was able to qualify for WIC, so I took all the help I could get while I was there. By April, I had to decide whether I wanted to stay in Hawaii or go elsewhere. I made the calculated decision to leave the island and took orders to Brunswick, Maine so that I could be closer to my family in New Jersey

Lesson #6: *Don't be afraid to ask for help. It's okay. We're human, and sometimes life happens, and we need a little hand to help us out. Be it government programs or family and friends, it's okay to ask for help. I was fortunate to have my mother and sisters help me with my daughter while I was serving in the Navy. Also, if a situationship is not serving you, leave. One thing about me is that I don't beg for anyone to love me. The people who love you will want to be with you unconditionally.*

CHAPTER 4

No Woman No Cry

I named this chapter "No Woman No Cry" because that's exactly what I did the entire year during my duty station in Maine. I cried a lot. I felt lonely and depressed. I was a single woman with a blessing in the form of a daughter, but I never wanted that to be my life. I wanted to have a family, but I had to face reality and stay strong for my daughter. I ended up renting a big house, and what a big mistake.

First, Maine is already very secluded, and in Topsham, even worse. Maine is so full of beautiful views of nature. The air was fresh and cool. But there was this utter solitude in comparison to tropical Hawaii. You wouldn't see people past 7 p.m. and stores closed early. By the grace of God, I didn't end up doing something crazy living so secluded. I think I had post-partum depression too, so the loneliness in Maine didn't help.

Despite how I was feeling, it was time to deploy. I made all preparations to leave my now nine-month-old daughter with my mother in New Jersey and put all my furniture in storage.

The per diem in El Salvador was a good amount of money, so I came up with a frugal plan to maximize my savings. While at the base, we weren't allowed to leave the hotel due to a previous command whose guys got into trouble, so we all faced the consequences. Word on the street was that they went to a red zone area where it was deemed dangerous, and they were assaulted by some locals.

While in El Salvador, I took the time to plan my exit strategy from the Navy. I made this decision because I had missed my daughter's first birthday, first Christmas, and her first steps. I said out loud, "I will *never* leave my child again!" I started saving all my per diem. I think I saved a little over twelve thousand dollars. I would only eat tuna on crackers with an apple for lunch and the same for dinner, and I would have a big breakfast at the hotel. I think I ran off the depression. I would run mile after mile in the hot ass sun, from the aircraft hangar to the main gate, and run it back. I lost so much weight that summer. I finally got rid of that baby weight.

I was fortunate to get the choice to leave deployment about a month earlier. I went to New Jersey to pick up my daughter, and when she first saw me, she ran away from me and called for "Mama!" but it wasn't me—she called for her grandmother. Four months! It took her four months to forget me. I immediately burst into tears. I couldn't believe that my baby would forget me so quickly. That was my epiphany that I had to end my time in the military. Decisions come with uncertainties, and I had to face new challenges. I had no place to live, no job, a car loan, bills, and a fourteen-month-old.

Lesson #7: Make your mental health a priority! I thought feeling this sense of overwhelm was normal. I don't recall anyone offering me information about how to treat post-partum depression, and I dealt with it on my own. I was never asked at medical how I felt or given any extra sup-port after giving birth to my daughter. If you relate, please seek medical or professional help, especially if you feel like harming yourself or need someone to talk to. There's no shame in asking for help. Also, be kind and empathetic to others. You don't know their situation or what they're going through.

Prior to getting out of the Navy, I had to figure out where I was going to live. My mother lived in a double-wide mobile home with my stepdad and three sisters, so there wasn't any room for me, my daughter, and my household items, which filled a two-story house. Fortunately, across the street from my mother's mobile home park, there was another mobile home park. I went over to check out the area, and I saw a single-wide home for sale for thirteen thousand dollars.

I immediately called the realtor on the for-sale sign, and we met up. I asked the seller's realtor to tell the seller that I had seven thousand dollars in *cash*. (I enunciated it. I think I learned it from someone who said to get someone to sell it cheaper, always offer cash, and over-emphasize it.) And guess what? Yes, the seller agreed, and I bought the house for seven thousand bucks. I was so relieved that I finally had a place to live. It was a two-bedroom mobile home. It needed some TLC, but that's okay. For me, it was temporary until I could figure my life out.

When I tell people that I lived in a mobile home, they always ask me, "Why didn't you apply for low-income housing?" Well, if you don't have a job, you don't even qualify for it. Low income in 2006 you would be paying for rent eight hundred to nine hundred fifty dollars a month. I couldn't afford to pay this plus other bills. After your military service is done, you're done. You must figure out what to do on your own, at least that's how it was for me. The military used to discharge you, and that's it. The system is much better now for veterans, but I wasn't that fortunate.

Lesson #8: You know that saying, "When life gives you lemons, make lemonade"? Well, that's exactly what I did. Most people I know would never live in a trailer park, but living in that mobile home was my leverage. I used that opportunity to save and take care of what was next to come.

The day came when I received my housing shipment from the storage facility. The moving company came and pretty much stuffed my single-wide mobile home with boxes. It was so overwhelming. I didn't know where to begin because we couldn't walk inside, just in the kitchen. My sister and I started opening boxes and sorting stuff. I don't recall exactly how long it took us to break down every box, but it must have been at least two weeks. I gave away my queen bed and patio set to a friend and his wife. Thinking about it now, I didn't sell anything, but I guess I didn't want to be bothered by selling. I just wanted to clear my house.

I started out paying $348 per month for the rent, which covered water and sewage plus land rental. That helped me out so much because you can't beat paying that much for rent in New Jersey. The unemployment office qualified me to receive $530 dollars a week that was allocated for my car loan, rent and utilities, food, baby formula, diapers, gas, and other bills. That wasn't enough money to live comfortably, and I needed to fix the mobile home because it wasn't in the best condition. I had to rip off the floors and replace them, repaint, redo the kitchen because it was old and disgusting, but the fact that I had my own place kept me going. I ended up raking up thirteen thousand dollars on my credit card. So now I had that credit bill to add to my previous list.

All the weight I had lost in El Salvador, I gained back and some. The stress and anxiety were high. I would cry, trying to figure out what the hell I was going to do. I said to myself, "I need a job. I can't sit around here for another six months collecting unemployment and do nothing. This is not me." So, I asked my aunt (uncle's ex-wife) to help me get a job at a cosmetic company she worked for.

I went to the interview and was offered twelve dollars an hour as a line leader. I looked at the hiring manager like he was crazy and got up and said, "I don't think this position is for me. I can't buy diapers making twelve dollars an hour.

I'm looking to make a minimum of sixteen dollars an hour. I have an associate degree, and I have six years of military experience."

So, I walked out and went home. You might be thinking, sixteen dollars is not much. I didn't care. I needed a job, and sixteen dollars was good for me at that time. The next day, I got a call from a supervisor at the same company who offered me an office position at sixteen dollars an hour, so I accepted.

Lesson #9: Know your worth. At that time, I wanted to make sixteen dollars an hour, so I wasn't going to take anything less. Have a clear picture of what you want and stick to it, no deviation allowed.

CHAPTER 5

Annuity What?

I started working at that cosmetic company in the fall of 2006. I was twenty-six years old. I really liked working at that company because I worked in an office, which was the opposite of what I had known in the past six years, working outdoors in the rain or snow, always dirty in coveralls. To top it off, I got free cosmetics. What woman doesn't like free cosmetics?

This was my first time getting introduced to the 401k. I took every bit of information that HR gave me about my benefits and read it to try to understand it. This company provided a match, so I simply invested in the match because that's all I could afford with my pay rate. So now I had an existing Roth which was on autopilot buying and holding since I was twenty-two, and now a 401k. I felt so proud of myself.

Unfortunately, I was still very naïve and uneducated about investing, and I had no idea where that money was being invested. I wanted some guidance from a professional financial advisor, so I called USAA, and they had a program called "Managed Portfolio," which charges you one percent for someone to manage your money.

The portfolio manager told me to take ten thousand dollars from my Roth and invest in an annuity. Lord, I had no idea what the hell an annuity was. I went with his explanation: "You don't want to put all your eggs in one basket." So, I gave him the okay. I couldn't take the money out for the next seven years and at the end of this term, I would get a crappy return. I think it was two percent, maybe less.

Lesson #10: Read, read, read. Your teachers would tell you to read and learn math because you'll need it. They were right. You need to read everything so that you can understand what you're getting into, especially when it's a legal document or something financial. If you don't understand, hire someone who can explain things to you in layman's terms. Otherwise, you'll have to go to your bank's financial advisor and trust that they're doing the right thing for you. I would have never taken money out of my Roth and put it in an annuity if I knew then what I know now. One percent is a lot of money, especially when it's a large amount. Knowledge is power, so if you put effort in educating yourself on investing, you won't need to pay one percent to have your money managed. You can manage it yourself.

CHAPTER 6

Good 'Ole 2008

While sitting on my oversized sofa, on my Sony VAIO laptop looking at my Roth IRA and 401k, all I could look at was the history chart of my portfolio. I had lost over forty-five thousand dollars, and my heart started racing. I almost went into full panic mode. The year was 2008 and all you would hear on the news and the people chattering about balloon mortgages and homes prices falling by ridiculous amounts. As a result, there were foreclosures and short sales all over the United States. Also buzzing was that the Dow had dropped more than two hundred points. What the hell was the Dow? I had an idea.

I just knew that the little chart line on my USAA investment account was extremely down, and that I'd lost thousands of my hard-earned invested dollars. Oh, the anxiety grew in me with the uncertainty of whether the market was going to completely crash, and I'd lose all my money. I was battling the decision to do what *everyone* does during these times, which is sell everything and keep what is left. But I'm glad that I didn't. Something inside of me told me not to, not to panic, that this was temporary. I'm glad that I listened to that inner voice because I wouldn't be writing this book if I did.

Lesson #11: Don't fear when the stock market is low or during times of uncertainty. It is okay. Keep buying and holding. Times like these are your best friend because you're buying at the lowest, and based on historical data, the stock market always goes back up. If you're between your twenties and thirties, time is your best friend. Tony Robbin's books, Money Master the Game and Unshakeable dive deeper into the psychology and fears of the market. I encourage you to check them out. Get an Audible for Money Master the Game because it's a six-hundred-page monster. You might want to listen to it instead.

During this time, I stumbled upon Dave Ramsey's baby steps. I read about his baby steps and thought to myself, *Wait a minute, I've been doing these baby steps since I was twenty-one.* Remember when I was living paycheck to paycheck? I saved a thousand dollars initially, then I had an emergency fund. Dave says to calculate your expenses and use that to save for your emergency fund. I had already done that as well. I agree with Dave, to align your numbers based on your monthly expenses so that you have those covered, but the more you save, the better. I think I was on baby step number four: invest fifteen percent of your household income in retirement and step five: pay off your home early around this time. I skipped step five because I wasn't thinking about saving any money for my daughter's education at this time. Again, this was due to the lack of knowledge and misinformation

I tried learning more about mutual funds because Dave Ramsey kept saying to invest in a mutual fund, and so I did. But once again, I had no clue how to read the prospectus for a mutual fund. (A prospectus is the document that has the fees and other important information about the fund that you're investing in.) I went on investing in a bunch of mutual funds without educating myself on what they were. I remember when the HR staff would hand me a piece of paper that listed all available funds to invest in, and I was told to allocate my money to whatever funds I'd like. Not knowing much, I just put percentages all over the place. but when I think about it, I lost so much money due to ignorance and of course, I didn't have anyone to teach me this stuff. I would try asking HR personnel, and I'd either get ignored, an attitude, or was told to read. I tried reading the documents, but this stuff was like reading a manuscript from another plate. What the hell's *expense ratio*? *Prospectus* what? I would give up and just leave my investment as it was.

CHAPTER 7

First Re-Strategizing Phase

The years 2006 to 2008 were the busiest years of my life. I was juggling a full-time job, full-time college, and being full-time Mommy. There was a point where I wanted to quit. I walked into my college advisor's office, and I told her I was ready to quit. She sat me down and gave me some options, and quitting wasn't one. I was fortunate enough to have professors that allowed me to bring my daughter to class.. I would stay up all night and fall asleep on my laptop working on research papers or taking an exam for my hybrid classes. All the sacrifice was worth it—by the grace of God, I was able to earn my Bachelor's in Technical Management in 2008.

After graduating, I decided that it was time to ask for more money at the cosmetic company. I Googled, "How to ask for more money at work?" So, I followed the guidelines from the blog: I presented my case to the director of the department and asked for a one-dollar increase or forty-five-thousand-dollar salary, but my request was declined, and I was told that that salary was for a supervisor. Are you kidding me? *One lousy dollar?* Fortunately, God always came through, and I got a call from DeVry's career center that there was a position available for a junior business analyst position in Princeton.

I was ecstatic! I remember sitting in my car during my lunchtime practicing my interviewing skills, looking in the mirror doing my own mock interviews. The hiring manager asked about batching—well, he was referring to payments. The craziest thing is that I was able to relate lipstick batching with payments batching. Somehow, I passed the phone interview and the face-to-face, and I was hired. Of course, I negotiated my salary, and I got three thousand dollars more than the initial offer.

It felt so good to hand in my resignation. I was entering a world that would forever change my life.

Lesson #12: This lesson aligns with Lesson #9: NEGO-TIATE your salary! How else are you going to Max It Out? By taking the first number the hiring manager throws at you? No way! Build that confidence. Know that you're the bomb. You can do that job. You know you'll be working super hard for the company when you're hired, so why not get paid what you're worth? More money means you'll be able to invest more and treat yourself more, so do it! Don't be afraid to negotiate. I've coached men and women to always negotiate. Negotiate personal time, money, stocks. If you go into an interview unprepared, you'll get the least.

Thanks to DeVry University, I was able to get my foot in the door in the FinTech (Financial Technology) space. I began working as a junior business analyst working on configuring and implementing billers onto the company's billing system among other responsibilities. I learned the system so fast. I had this hunger for success and an urgency to make more money due to my living conditions.

I developed a friendship with a project manager at this company. He told me not to put too much emphasis on being a veteran in the private sector, that civilians don't care about the military. I was shocked but took his advice. He saw that I had many questions about the system and the work that I was doing. He told me to see Joanie, that she was the go-to person at the company.

I created a list of questions and scheduled a one-on-one meeting with her. This woman was a genius. She retained so much information and knew how to regurgitate it like it was the ABCs. . She asked me, "How long have you been working here?"

"Just a month," I said.

"You know more than the people who've been working here for years," she said. She even emailed my manager and told her the same.

I still have that email to this day. I felt proud of myself. From that point on, I knew that I could do just about anything.

One day, I received a letter from my previous employer that I had a few options I could do with my old 401k: I could leave it there, or I could roll it over into a Rollover IRA. Thanks to Google, I read everything about a Rollover IRA, so I proceed to do the paperwork. This process is a pain, but I'm glad I did it. I had investments in three different brokerage firms: Vanguard, Fidelity, and USAA. It was so overwhelming to track and keep up with, so I decided to put everything in one location. I chose USAA.

Lesson #13: Consolidate all 401k. Guys and gals, stop being lazy and roll over those 401k's, especially if you've had multiple jobs. I say "lazy" because I know a lot of people who don't want to go through the process of consolidating. I know that the paperwork can be tedious but damn it, it feels good to have all your money in one location. Pick Vanguard or Fidelity, open a Rollover IRA, and once you have that account open, get the rollover paperwork from your company and roll it over. I personally find Fidelity more user-friendly, and they offer electronic rollover so there's no excuse. The best part is that you can see the charts of your money as it grows.

While working at the new company, I decided to max out the Roth IRA contributions, which was five thousand dollars a year, and I did up to the match in my 401k. I began listening to Audibles. The first book was *The Automatic Millionaire* by David Bach. The book was good, and I was doing exactly what he suggested years ago, which was to have the money automatically debited from your account and invested into your Roth IRA and other investments. I should have written a book back then, but I guess I wasn't ready yet. My love for self-improvement books grew from that time forward.

CHAPTER 8

Ghosted and Scared

I'm not going to lie, I'm a very humble person. However, living in a mobile home has its advantages and disadvantages. Although I was able to save money and pay off many of my debts, there were some social and emotional disadvantages to this.

Let me tell you of the time I got ghosted, which I had *never* experienced before. I went out to dance Latin music one night, and my eyes locked with this really good looking guyI was automatically attracted to him. We exchanged numbers, and we began texting and talking on the phone. He told me he was going to school to be a dentist, that he had so much respect for single mothers as his mother was a single mom herself. Well, he asked me out on a date. I accepted, and we met at a local sports bar.

After the date, he drove me to show me the home where his uncle lived, and he talked about his plan of owning a big home. It was getting late so he took me back to my house..

He wanted to see my mobile home but in the back of my head, I felt a bit insecure because I wasn't sure what he would think of me if he saw where I lived. I was going to school and had a good job with a better salary than before, and I knew that that mobile home was temporary. I thought to myself, *Well, he seems humble, and he talked so much about how he respected single mothers, so why not? I'll let him see where I live.* We got to my house. I opened the door, but my sister and daughter were sleeping in the living room, so we didn't go in. We hugged , he said he would call or text me and he left. The following week, I didn't hear from him. I texted, called, and emailed, and nothing. *Have I been ghosted? Why?* Then I thought, *Oh, he discriminated against me because of where I live. Wait, maybe he thought I was a gold-digger?* I never heard from him ever again. I'm not going to lie, that hurt like hell. It hurt because I wished that I could have lived in a better place, but that was all I could afford at the time. I mean it could have been that he just wasn't interested but, in my head, it was because I lived in a mobile home, so that got embedded in my subconscious. I took it as another lesson for growth.

Lesson #14: Ghosting is a coward's way to say, "We're not a match" or "There's no connection." In this case, I truly believe that he got turned off from seeing my mobile home. Regardless of his reasons, being ghosted should not be taken personally. Being ghosted fueled my desire to make a change. I turned that negative experience into a positive one, so I shifted my focus to saving for a house.

This next experience added more fuel to the fire. One winter day, my daughter and I were getting ready to go to sleep. We heard scratching, meowing, and hissing sounds coming from the heat vents in our mobile home. I thought there were cats in the vents, but nope, they were possums. Apparently, the skirting on the home had areas where wild animals went in to find warmth during harsh Jersey winter months.

My daughter started shaking and screaming, "I want to go to Guita's house! I want to go to Guita's house!" "Guita" for her was saying "abuela" which means "grandma" in Spanish. I've never seen my daughter shake like that. She had so much fear in her eyes that it made me pack up, and off we went to my mom's mobile home across the highway.

I cried that night and thought, *I'm a terrible mom. How could I continue living here? My daughter is about to start school, and she's going to get picked on by the rich kids in the area. I need to do something about this.*

I remembered something that my sister Jennifer said to me: "Brenda, it's so embarrassing to get off the bus. Those kids that live in those rich houses scream out of the window, 'You live in a coke can!' Or 'You're trailer trash!' You need to get a house or an apartment so she doesn't get bullied."

Her words stuck, so I began saving as much money as possible for a house. I didn't go on vacation for the next few years until I paid off all my debts and planned on saving a minimum of five thousand dollars and planned on selling my mobile home for six thousand dollars. I made this my primary focus, and with every income tax refund I would pay towards my debts, I would split my refund for vacation and the other half would pay off debt. Depending on the goal, I would split half or just pay the entire refund. Any bonus from work, I threw it towards the debt, then into savings. When it comes to debt, my thought is that if you owe it, pay it and clear that from your checklist first.

Lesson #15: When paying off debt such as credit cards and loans, tackle the ones with the smallest amount first, then the one with the highest annual percentage rate. This is what I personally did and the advice I give when I mentor someone. See the table below:

Type of Debt	Amount owed	Annual APR	Rank
Visa	$500.00	18%	First
American Express	$5500.00	12%	Second
Car Loan	$28,900	3.99%	Third
Mortgage	$250,000	6%	Fourth

I eventually paid off all my debt. Today, I call debt "investments." It's a psychological thing for me. "Debt" sounds more negative, like I'm drowning in debt, so going forwards, call them "investments." Investments sound more positive because whatever you bought with that money, you invested that in yourself. My credit card investment was used to fix that mobile home, to pay for books, and yes, to treat myself occasionally.

It was now time to start selling my mobile home, and I thought that was going to be challenging. *Who would buy a mobile home? I mean, I did, but most people have a misconception about mobile homes.* I knew of a couple who had two kids, and they were technically homeless. They were staying in hotels, so I told a friend to let them know that I would sell them the mobile home for five thousand dollars. Their feedback was that they would never live in a trailer park. They said, "Not with those kinds of people."

I couldn't believe what I was hearing. I mean, they had nowhere to live with their two kids. The mobile home park had two beautiful playgrounds where my daughter played. My neighbors were so kind and just nice, humble people. This was the disadvantage of living in a mobile home: the social stigma and discrimination. I felt highly offended. Well, a few months later, I sold it to a newly married young couple for five thousand dollars.

Lesson #16: Be humble and stay humble throughout your journey in life. Remember the couple who rejected the offer to buy my mobile home? Well, that family fell apart, the kids were sent to their grandmothers and the wife passed away.

CHAPTER 9

Speak Up!

Prior to selling the mobile home and buying a new house, I was in the process of changing jobs. I was caught in the middle of work bureaucracy as well, a departmental warfare which brought me to tears every time I came home. My co-worker (the army veteran) tried several times to get me into his project management department but my manager blocked me from getting hired, someone told me that was the reason for not getting picked. A few months later, I tried to apply for a quality assurance position. The QA manager and I built a great rapport, and he wanted to hire me, but once again, I was told that my manager had blocked it. I felt terrible. Why me? How does a company expect you to stick around when there's no growth? I sucked it up and just continued doing excellently at my current position and being patient.

We had an all-hands meeting. The VP asked a question, and I had my rulebook. I decided to raise my hand and answer the question. Later that day, my manager called me into the office to tell me that I had been picked by him to lead a migration project. I was extremely surprised since I was the new kid on the block, technically, even at one and a half years in the company. I was a bit skeptical about this, but I do what I'm told (coming from a military mindset).

It was hell on earth for like a month or two. My manager would ask me about the workload of this new team because she didn't see any work happening. Then I would ask the project manager in charge of that team when I would get work because my manager kept asking. He told me that I should not worry about it, that I had been assigned to that team. This went on and on. I was so stressed, and it started taking a toll on me.

To make matters worse, we were undergoing an acquisition, and the new CTO asked me to sit in a group to collaborate in a Q&A so he could understand all of the teams' processes. My manager sent me an email to tell me that the team valued me with no hidden agenda and that my performance would be affected if I didn't disclose all of my meetings with the CTO.

I felt my stomach sink, like someone had punched me hard right on the gut. *Why would he say this to me? He wants me to tell him every time I meet with the CTO? But he knows where we meet. Why can't he just go?* Those were my thoughts. I cried that day. I wasn't sure what to do. My supervisor wanted to dissipate this new team, then the senior wanted to send me that nasty little email.

I had enough. I was ready to quit, so I walked into the VP's office and just poured my heart out. "I'm a single parent. I just need to do the work I need to do for this company, get paid, and go home. I don't know who picked me to be in this team, but I don't want it if they're going to stress me out." I told her about how they had me going back and forth with my manager and the PMO manager, and to top it off, I got an email from my Senior director that my performance would be affected if I held any secret meetings.

When told he did that, she was shocked! She asked me to send her that email and that I was doing a great job, and I shouldn't worry, that my email was the icing on the cake for the case they already had on the director. *Oh my God, what have I done?* I thought. *I'm sure going to get fired now.*

A few weeks later, while I was working, we heard our director making these grunting noises and saying, "I'm being asked to go to HR."

One of my co-workers jokingly said, "Are you getting fired?"

My stomach sank again. I felt really bad. I wasn't sure what was happening until an hour later when we heard the key fob no longer worked. He banged on the door, and we let him in. Yup, he just got fired. I felt guilty and at the time relieved that there would be no more Boss Bully. Eleven years later, I found out that he had done this to all of his employees, which was why they had a case on him. That gave me closure that I had done the right thing.

Lesson #17: Speak up! Closed mouths don't get fed. Being a veteran with military training sometimes hinders us. I used to never speak up to my leaders. We have to do what we are told else we get punished. This conditioning began in bootcamp. Forget about the open-door policy; that was not allowed. You'd face some good yelling and God knows what else. At least that is how it was during my time in the service. Also coming from a family that would embed into our kid's brains, "Don't get into adult conversations. Who are you to speak up?" followed with a good beating. Yeah, I never spoke up. When you've had enough, you must speak up. Speak up even before you've reached that breaking point, no matter the consequences. Just speak up!

A new job opportunity presented itself. My co-worker, Miles, asked me if I wanted to interview for a project manager role at another company. I gave him a resounding "YES!" At the interview, the hiring manager asked me some very deep questions. Having little project management experience, which I had disclosed, she told me that I didn't interview well as a project manager, but she would give me an opportunity to start as a project coordinator, and she would pay me fifty-two thousand dollars.

I felt my insides boil, but I respectfully declined and said, "I'm afraid that's less than a lateral move for me."

"Well, I still want you to work with us," she said. "Perhaps you're interested in business analysis."

My eyes lit up because it was a way to leverage my already obtained experience.

I interviewed for the business analyst position and was hired. Once again, I negotiated my salary, and I was given three thousand dollars more than what I had originally asked for. What a blessing! I had increased my salary a little over twenty thousand dollars in two and a half years. That was a huge deal for me.

This new company was a startup. I was handed a laptop, and it was a sink-or-swim situation. At first, I was a bit scared that I wasn't going to understand anything. Listening to my coworkers when they talked about the product would make my stomach sink. *What are they saying? I feel like I'm on another planet.* I was assigned a project with another minority coworker; at the time there were only three minorities working there. I told him, "Don't worry, I'm going to figure this out, and I'll teach it to you."

I scheduled a meeting with one of the Business Analysts who was very knowledgeable, and we drilled him with questions. After a few rounds of sessions with different coworkers, I finally understood the product to a point that I no longer felt like a new resident on planet Mars.

I cried several times at this job. There were times where I felt like I had to learn everything and prove myself, while others did nothing. There were only a few of us who truly wanted to learn, and many times you had to learn it yourself because no one had the patience to teach you. It was more nerve-racking because you had to go in front of a client, and you were the expert, so the client expected you to be able to answer their questions.

One day, I stumbled upon someone's offer letter. This person made over thirty thousand dollars more than me—same title but different genders. I was livid! Imagine: had I not negotiated my salary, I would have been making even less money. That's when I realized that with my knowledge, skills, and abilities, I could make thirty thousand dollars more. I kept this information to myself and just kept learning, working, and focusing on house-hunting because I needed to give my daughter better living conditions.

Lesson #18: From experience, a way to increase your salary is by switching jobs. If your job isn't fulfilling you, challenging you, or you don't feel valued or appreciated, then change your job. Women, especially, we still make eighty-three cents to every dollar a man makes, so make sure that you negotiate as said in Lesson #12 and move jobs if you must ..

CHAPTER 10

Started from the Bottom

No one told me how stressful looking for a house would be. I took a free first-time homeowner course from the county I was living in. As you can probably already tell, I love educating myself. I love learning and knowing the dos and don'ts of anything major that I'm about to step into. I did so much research and late nights trying to figure out what I wanted my first home to be like and what to expect as a new homeowner. So, I heard about short sale homes, and I thought, *If I could get a short sale, I would fix it up, and it'll be worth a lot more in the long run.* I looked at several regular priced single-family homes, townhomes, and then came the short sales. A short sale means the property's asking price is less than the amount due on the current owner's mortgage.

During my home hunting, some of these short sales were destroyed. One townhome had paint splashed all over the walls. I could feel the anger left behind in that home. Another home had extreme damage to the walls, broken windows, and doors. I could feel the negative energy and the owner's disappointment of losing their home. This was during the 2008 to 2011 balloon mortgages time, where people were paying only the interest rate of their mortgage loan and not their mortgage principle. So, the principle just accumulated, and it hit them like a ton of bricks when they found out how much they owed. Terrible!

This is the power of education! You see why I strive to read and understand what I'm getting into?

This brings me to tell you about my first experience in submitting a home offer. I went to see the house. First, I was worried about how far it would be from my job and how it would affect my daughter's transportation. Would I be able to put her on the bus? Would I be able to drive her and pick her up? The house was okay. It was a two-story colonial, with a huge backyard, but it had no fence. During our walk, I could smell gas or something weird in the air. The basement was unfinished, and it looked pretty dark, and it smelled damp. It reminded me of that movie *Arachnophobia*—just cobwebs everywhere.

I ended up putting an offer on it that same Friday afternoon. I remember lying in bed that night thinking that I made a mistake, thinking how awful that house was, and a whiff of gas came into my nose. I swear the brain is so powerful that it made me jump out of bed with my heart pounding and me thinking, *I need to pull out of that contract. That house smelled like gas, and I don't want it.* I imagined that house having a gas leakage, so my stomach started to ache, and I began to heave. I started hyperventilating, and I squatted in a fetal position thinking, *I'm making a big mistake. I don't want that house. I need to retract that offer.* So, I immediately emailed that realtor and told her to please pull the offer. My realtor told me that because it was the weekend, she hadn't submitted the paperwork. Phew! It was like a bucket of cold water was thrown on me. Thank God!

After that ordeal, I was so embarrassed that I changed realtors. I ended up hiring April. She was a single parent, and she was so nice. By then, I had a clear idea of what kind of house I wanted: a three-bedroom, short sale. We looked at many until we stumbled upon a three-bedroom, two-bath Cape Cod. There were squatters who had broken into the house, so it needed a new back door, windows, and the backyard was a complete jungle and hot mess, overtaken by the wild vines that wrapped around trees and basically anything it touched. I didn't feel as much anxiety as I did with the first house, so I put the bid in.

It was August 11, 2011, and we got hit with one of the worst hurricanes we've ever experienced: Irene. It devastated and flooded the Caribbean and the East Coast. I was staying temporarily in a friend's basement studio, and all our stuff got flooded. We elevated my things, and we didn't sleep all night long trying to keep the water from coming in. I think everyone in NJ got flooded that year. It was terrible. I wanted to cry because I thought, *Oh, if the house got flooded, the bank isn't going to approve my loan.* Well, the inspection did show that it had gotten flooded but quickly remediated. Everything seemed to be okay, and the bank approved my loan. I was happy despite what we had just endured.

In twelve years of living in this house, I've had to remove and replace the water heater twice, my house got broken into and all electronics were stolen, my basement was flooded three times, main line backed up twice, sum pump in the basement bathroom replaced, installed a French drain and sump pump in the basement, a French drain outside, had four trees removed, backyard completely redone, replaced windows and two doors, redid the kitchen because it had black mold, fixed insulation in the attic, replaced the garage door and other small repairs—too many to mention. This was approximately twenty to twenty-five thousand dollars spent on repairs. Granted, I bought the house for a hundred forty thousand, and it's now worth approximately three hundred fifty thousand dollars, so I'm still positive in equity. Even though I've had a few headaches, I'm glad that I had the opportunity to buy a short sale.

Lesson #19 – Buying a short sale is not for the faint of heart. If you're not mentally prepared to own a fixer-upper, then don't do it. Things start breaking down out of nowhere, and you had better be prepared to fix it. Pay for a good home inspector and have them stick a camera in the main sewer line. Check the basement and drainage of the home, and make sure the roof is inspected. Those are some of the major things I would check on in my next home. Make sure you have that emergency fund with at least ten thousand dollars saved up.

To be quite frank, being a single mother and trying to manage the house, bills, a career, and school hasn't been easy. At times, I've wanted to give up. I've been drained mentally, emotionally, and spiritually, but when you have a child, that mother gene kicks in and you keep going. God gave me the strength to keep going, and so I did.

CHAPTER 11

Second Re-Strategizing Phase

My commute was one hour to and from work, so instead of listening to music or talking to people on the phone, I would listen to audiobooks. I don't recall how I stumbled upon the book, *Simple Path to Wealth*, but it was a game changer for me. The author prefers Vanguard and explains how he invested with his wife and did the same for his daughter. This book was my starting point on learning about expense ratios and how mutual funds were fee-eaters. I immediately started reallocating my money from mutual funds to index funds. It felt so good to feel more in control of your own investments.

I also kicked to the curb the Managed Portfolio from USAA. They charged a one percent fee to manage my money, but I had no idea if they were making me money or not. Every year they would call me to let me know that after fees, I still made money. I took their word for it. However, something in me always felt uneasy, so I took matters into my own hands.

One day while scrolling through Instagram I found Personal Finance Club's page. Jeremy Schneider was the man behind this page, and his information was so educational. I ended up bingeing and scrolling through his entire page. By now I've learned that index funds are the funds that the most famous investors recommend investing in. *Warrant Buffett, JL Collins, and now Jeremy? Okay, I need to re-strategize ASAP!* I thought.

I was unsure if my funds were allocated properly so I DM-ed Jeremy hoping he would respond. I wanted him to look at my investments and suggest what I needed to adjust. Holy crap! Jeremy responded and didn't hesitate to ask me for my list of funds. We set up a date to talk.

The first thing he pointed out was the annuity I had. He wondered why I had invested in that. I told him about the USAA fund manager who had told me the story of not putting all my eggs in one basket, so I put ten thousand dollars in an annuity without knowing what it was. Lucky me, I only had three months left in that annuity agreement. I had to hold it for seven years, or else I would get a penalty for early withdrawal. I think I only earned a little over two percent for those seven years—what a rip off! That's the consequence of being ignorant in the world of personal finance. He also mentioned that I had several mutual funds which had high fees, so I moved those into low cost index funds. I had a few index funds, so I kept those there.

After that day, I started feeling more confident about what I need to look at when choosing which funds to invest in. I use an Excel spreadsheet to keep track of all my funds. I know there are apps out there like Empower, previously known as Personal Capital. I don't like giving them access to my account numbers, so I prefer tracking them on Excel.

Lesson #20 – Make a list of all your accounts and funds—every single one. You can use this to see what you currently own and where you've invested your money, plus you'll see what fees you're paying on each fund. I've included the list I use on Excel to track all my accounts. I've modified the data for this example:

Broker	Account type	Fund	Description	Gross Expense Ratio	Net Expense Ratio	Amount	Date Checked	Comment
Merryl Lynch	401k	VTRS45	Vanguard Target Retirment Trust Select 20455	0.05%		$ 40,000.00	4/11/2023	
Fidelity	Roth IRA	FIOFX	Fidelity Freedom Index 245 Investor	0.12%	0.12%	$ 55,670.00	4/11/2023	
Fidelity	Rollover IRA	DGEAX	NY Mellon Global Emerging Markets Fund - Class	1.30%	1.25%	$ 30,690.00	4/11/2023	
Fidelity	Cash Account	PRCIX	T. Rowe Price New Income Fund	0.44%	0.44%	$ 10,103.36	4/11/2023	
Fidelity	Brokerage Account	FIOFX	Fidelity Freedom Index 245 Investor	0.12%	0.12%	$ 18,561.54	4/11/2023	
Ally	Brokerage Account	n/a	Stocks	-	-	$ 600.00	4/11/2023	
TSP	Lifecycle	L2045	L Funds Lifecycle Funds	0.01%	0.04%	$ 3,300.00	4/11/2023	
HSA						$ 6,500.00	4/13/2023	
Fidelity	Annuity	FPVAC	Fidelity VIP FundsManager 60	0.80%	0.75%	10,00	4/16/2023	Annuity chargeof 1.90% and Surrender Fee of 7%
TOTAL						$ 158,924.90		

As you can see in the table, the DGEAX NY Mellon Global Emerging Markets Fund has a gross expense ratio of 1.30% and net expense ratio of 1.25%. Think about it. What would you rather pay in fees? Let's calculate: 1.30% of $100,000 = $1,300 versus 0.12% of $10,000 = $12. I don't know about you, but I would rather pay twelve bucks in fees per year than $1,300.

Okay, so now it's your turn to do this exercise. If you have funds, list them all. Don't proceed to the next chapter. Do it now, or else you won't do it. You can print the My Funds Tracking Spreadsheet included at the end of this book, or you can create your own using Excel. But do it. Now go Max It Out!

I went ahead and re-strategized, rebalanced my accounts, and made sure I was investing in low-cost index funds. There are thousands of investment funds you can choose from, and this can be overwhelming. So, depending on your risk level, whether you want to self-manage or have it done automatically for you, there are several strategies you can use to start investing. If you don't want to hire a financial advisor and you don't want to manage and rebalance the funds yourself, then you can choose a target-date index fund. What is a target-date index fund? In layman's terms, it's an index fund that has a mix of investments.

Let's use fruits. Suppose apples were all U.S stocks index funds, oranges are international stocks index funds, and pears are bonds index funds. You can buy individual apples, pears, and oranges, and when you have too many of one fund, you have to rebalance based on your risk level. With a target-date index fund, you get all three fruits, and they are allocated based on your retirement date.

If you start investing in your twenties or thirties, the target-date fund will invest more in stocks and a small percentage in non-stocks items like bonds. As you get closer to your retirement date, it automatically adjusts by investing less in risky stocks and more in bonds. Figure 1 below shows Fidelity Freedom 2055 Funds and how it adjusts as it gets closer to the year 2055. Some people may not agree with these kinds of funds, but they are like the funds offered in your 401k, plus you have to start somewhere and until you get comfortable with financial terms and navigating your brokerage firm's website, this is a good place to start for a but only you can make this decision.

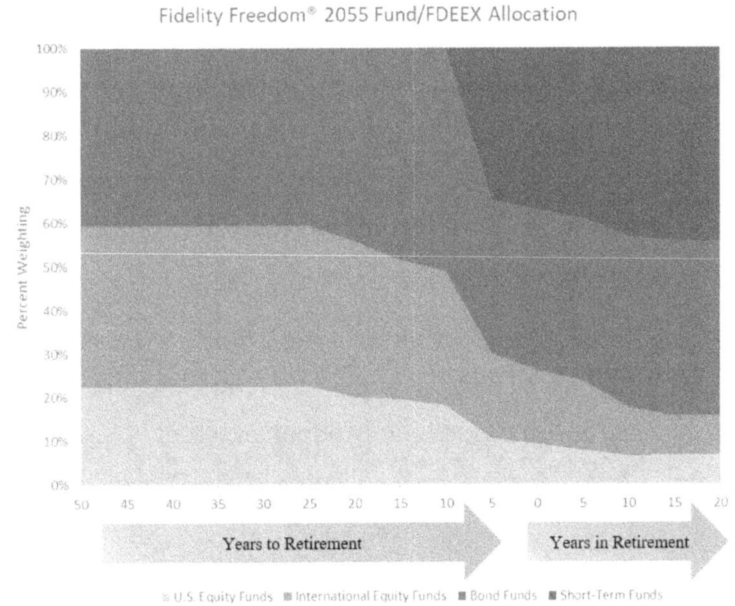

Source: Fidelity Freedom 20255 Fund/FDEEX Allocation from Fidelity.com

Now, if you're a hands-on investor like me, then you can invest in separate funds. The typically recommended strategy is to invest in three buckets: bucket one is domestic stocks, bucket two is international stocks, and bucket three is bonds.

Bucket One: Domestic stocks historically have a higher risk and higher returns. It is recommended to invest fifty-four percent on domestic stocks. Example stocks in this bucket are Amazon, Apple, Meta, and Tesla.

Bucket Two: International stocks. It is recommended to invest thirty-six percent here. Example stocks in this bucket are Taiwan Semiconductor MFG Co Ltd., Nestle SA, and Samsung Electronics Co. Ltd.

Bucket Three: Bonds are basically you lending money to a company, municipality, state or some other government entity and you get a percentage return. These are considered safer to invest in. It is recommended that you invest ten percent in bonds.

I've researched these different index funds from different brokerage firms. Each table represents a bucket as described above. A three-fund portfolio can look like this:

U.S STOCK MARKET:

Brokerage Firm	Stock Symbol	Fund Name
Fidelity	FZROX	Fidelity ZERO® Total Market Index Fund
Vanguard	VTSAX	Vanguard Total Stock Market Index Fund Admiral Shares
Schwab	SWTSX	Schwab Total Stock Market Index Fund
T.Rowe Price	POMIX	T. Rowe Price Total Equity Market Index Fund

INTERNATIONAL STOCKS:

Brokerage Firm	Stock Symbol	Fund Name
Fidelity	FZILX	Fidelity ZERO® International Index Fund
Vanguard	VTIAX	Vanguard Total International Stock Index Fund Admiral Shares
Schwab	SWISX	Schwab International Index Fund®
T. Rowe Price	PIEQX	T. Rowe Price International Equity Index Fund

BONDS:

Brokerage Firm	Stock Symbol	Fund Name
Fidelity	FXNAX	Fidelity® U.S. Bond Index Fund
Vanguard	VBTLX	Vanguard Total Bond Market Index Fund Admiral Shares
Schwab	SWAGX	Schwab U.S. Aggregate Bond Index Fund
T.Rowe Price	PBDIX	T. Rowe Price QM U.S. Bond Index Fund

If you have a total of ten thousand dollars you want to invest, you will need to pick one fund from each of the tables above depending on your choice of brokerage firm. What would I do in this case? I have Fidelity, so I would pick FZROX, FZILX, and FXNAX. I would allocate those ten thousand dollars for aggressive growth as follows:

FZROX: 54% of $10,000 = $5,400 goes to Bucket One

FZILX: 36% of $10,000 = $3,600 goes to Bucket Two

FXNAZ: 10% of $10,000 = $1,000 goes to Bucket Three

Personally, I invest in target-date index funds for some accounts. In others accounts, I use the three-fund portfolio. If this is your first time investing, you may want to start by using Fidelity and Vanguard DIY investment tools. In Fidelity, it is called Robo Investing Plus Advice, and in Vanguard it's called Digital Advisor. You basically answer a few questions, and based on your responses, the system will display the funds they recommend for you to invest in. Keep in mind to check the fees for each fund that you pick.

Where do you find those pesky fees I keep talking about? Do you remember the word *prospectus* or that disclosure document I mentioned earlier which we always throw in the garbage and never read? Well, you can find the fund fees in that document.

Look at the data of a random fund below. Holy moly! The expense ratio is 6.81% and net expense is still high at two percent. Additionally, it has a deferred load, which is a sales charge or fee that is assessed when an investor sells certain classes of the fund's shares before a specified date. So basically, you pay two percent in fees when you sell this fund. Would you invest in this fund knowing that? I know I wouldn't.

Morningstar Category	Small Blend
Fund Inception	09/30/2009
Exp Ratio (Gross) 01/27/2023	6.81%
Exp Ration (Net) 01/27/2023	2%
NAV 04/20/2023	$11.29
Deferred Load	1.00%
Minimum to Invest	$2,500.00
Turnover Rate 09/30/2022	29%
Portfolio Net Assets (SM) 03/31/2023	$117.89
Share Class Net Assets (SM) 03/31/2023	$0.25
12 Month Low-High 03/31/2023	$9.50 - $11.88

Source: Random Small Blend Fund Data from Fidelity

Now let's take a look at a target-date 2050 index fund. The expense ratio is only 0.49% and there are no other fees associated with this fund. The minimum to invest is zero, nada, zilch.

Second Re-Strategizing Phase

Morningstar Category	Target-Date 2050
Fund Inception	05/11/2023
Exp Ratio (Gross) 01/27/2023	0.49%
Exp Ration (Net) 01/27/2023	0.49%
NAV 04/20/2023	$10.11
Minimum to Invest	$0.00

Source: Fidelity Target-Date 20250 Data from Fidelity

Here's another index fund from Fidelity:

Morningstar Category	Large Blend
Fund Inception	08/02/2018
Exp Ratio (Gross) 01/27/2023	0.00%
Exp Ration (Net) 01/27/2023	0.00%
NAV 04/20/2023	$14.59
Minimum to Invest	$0.00
Turnover Rate 09/30/2022	3%
Portfolio Net Assets (SM) 03/31/2023	$13,935.57
12 Month Low-High 03/31/2023	$12.64 - $15.17

Source: Random Large Blend Fund Data from Fidelity

Answer the following questions from the above data:

Q1: What is the expense ratio on the fund?

Q2: What is the minimum to invest in this fund?

Okay, don't hate me for what I'm about to have you do. I'm a firm believer that people learn by doing and researching. Part of learning is acquiring knowledge through reading and listening, but the other part is practical. So, here's a little exercise for you. I want you to do this right now. Don't continue reading this book. Stop and do this exercise. Google the following and write it down what it generates:

What does "turnover rate" mean in an index fund?

What does "fund inception" mean?

What does "NAV" on an index fund mean?

Find two low-fee index funds for each of the following: U.S stocks, international stocks, and bonds.

I really hope this exercise helps you understand more about what to look for in an index fund or any mutual fund or ETF. Don't let this book become knowledge. Master this by doing it yourself.

CHAPTER 12

Max It Out

From 2011 to present day 2023, I decided to max out everything. As my salary increased, so did the amount of my retirement accounts contributions. As my accounts grew throughout the years, so did my mindset. All I could think of was to invest as much as possible, so I began maxing out my 401k, Roth IRA, and HSA. All the fear of the market and investing went away. I was on a different wavelength at that point. I've acquired sufficient knowledge to feel confident that my investments will keep growing until I decide to retire.

I want to touch a little bit on the HSA (Health Savings Account). So, an HSA account comes with a high deductible medical plan from your employer. It is a savings account, and you can invest the money as well. You can choose index funds within the HSA and voila, you're investing it and making more money for your medical bills. You can withdraw the money tax-free as long as the money is used for medical expenses—things like copayments and coinsurance. Go to hsastore.com to see a list of eligible items that also qualify for you to purchase.

Did you know you can buy a massage gun with your HSA savings account? Yes, you can. An HSA also has a maximum contribution limit and in the year 2023 for self-only its $3,850 and $7,750 for family. Be aware that every year it may increase, so check for your current year. There are so many rules for different situations, so I want you to research what an HSA is on YouTube or Google and read more about it.

In 2023, I'm still learning, reading, and recently started coaching one on one. I finished reading Tony Robbin's six-hundred-page book called, *Money Master the Game*. It took me three months to read it, and most of the things he wrote about, I had already done in my twenties and thirties. I did learn three new things about money from this book. First, I learned about was the All-Weather or All-Seasons Portfolio

So I did some digging, and this portfolio emerged in 1996 by Ray Dalio, an American billionaire investor and hedge fund manager. He served as co-chief investment officer of the world's largest hedge fund, Bridgewater Associates. This portfolio is supposed to do well in "all seasons, all weather." I was a bit surprised at how low the stock allocation and how high the bonds were. In my opinion, this allocation is for those who are more on the conservative side. I personally prefer being a little riskier, but this is all a personal choice.

Second, I learned about hiring a fiduciary. In layman's terms, a fiduciary works for the interests of the client unlike a

Financial Advisor. I honestly have to look more into this since I've experienced working with a Financial Advisor from USAA bank, as mentioned in an earlier chapter. In my opinion, a beginner investor shouldn't need to hire a fiduciary yet. But it is something that I encourage you to research before making a decision to hire one. Just make sure that they charge you a flat fee not a yearly percentage.

Third, I learned about FIA (Fixed Indexed Annuity). I know that in an earlier chapter a Financial Advisor advised me to put my money on a traditional annuity which gives you a small percentage after holding it for 7 years. I made a list of the pros and cons of an FIA:

Pros:

- ➢ Your principal – the money you invested is protected when the market goes down
- ➢ Your gains are based on the market index gains without exposing your principle – your money is not directly invested in the market
- ➢ Your gains are tax-deferred and compounds annually
- ➢ Death benefit – ensures that your beneficiaries receive a specified amount which is usually the initial premium or a higher value in the event of your death
- ➢ There is no annual contribution

Cons:

- ➢ Complex – understanding the terms, conditions and other components can be challenging.

> ➤ Caps and Participation Rates – so if the market index is doing 8% return, you may only get up to your specified cap which may be lower than 8%.
> ➤ Surrender charges – fees charged when you withdraw money within a certain period.
> ➤ Fees and Expenses – need to check the fees and costs
> ➤ Limited Liquidity – contains restrictions during the surrender charge period so it's not a good place to put your emergency money in

I personally would not consider an FIA or any type of annuity. Perhaps if I become a multi-millionaire or I find a reliable fiduciary then I'll consider it. I don't have enough knowledge about FIA's, so I don't feel comfortable investing in one. The way I will tackle this new piece of information is by reading more about it through repetition and try to understand it so that in the near future I can perhaps consider it as an investment tool. I encourage you to do the same.

Remember that the key to long-term investing is 'knowledge', I wish I had this book when I had just started my investing journey. Once you're done with this book, start another one until it registers in your brain. Think about this, how does the most successful golfer or basketball player become great at what he/she does, through repetition. Same goes with investing or anything else you do in life, if you practice every day, the more you'll master it. Eventually leading you in throwing away the 'fear' that has kept holding you back on starting your investment journey and on your way to Maxing It Out!

CHAPTER 13

The Secret to Wealth

On June 1st, 2021, I entered a cycle of anxiety that I had *never* experienced in my life. I'm contemplating on writing a book about it and how I overcame it. In the meantime, let me share with you how I felt at that point in my life. I had entered what they call the cycle of anxiety. I had so many intrusive thoughts, like, *What's the point of having it all? What's the point of having this house? I have this new job which is what I've always wanted, but I don't feel happy. I can't live like this!* It was something I wouldn't wish upon my worst enemy. But I got out of it and let me tell you, this brings me the secret to wealth: GRATITUDE!

I learned this from Tony Robbins. What's the point of having money and all the wealth in the world when you are questioning yourself? You get to the point where you don't want to live anymore. No amount of money makes you happy. So many people who are super rich end up committing suicide because they are miserable. I remember visiting family and going to a friend's home who were very poor but were so happy with the little that they had. These people would not eat to give you their last meal. Now *that's* happiness. You have to be grateful for what you already have so that when you do become wealthy, you maintain that same level of gratitude.

If my mental state was how it was in 2021, no amount of money would have made me happy, trust me. That's how deep in the rabbit hole I was. I've been practicing gratitude and maintaining a beautiful state for the past two years, and it has made a tremendous difference.

That being said, I'm truly grateful and thankful that you have allowed me to share my financial journey and life experiences with you. I send you blessings and best wishes in your investment journeys.

CHAPTER 14

Scenarios

The following scenarios are examples of how I would approach different situations when it comes to investing. I personally didn't invest in a 401k in my early to mid-twenties because I was in the military, and they don't provide a match, but they did offer a TSP (Thrift Savings Plan). I invested like one percent back in the early 2000s, but, since 2018, the military automatically enrolls military personnel by deducting three percent of their basic salary.

Before getting into the scenarios, here's a check list for order of investing:

- ➢ 401k invest up to the match.
- ➢ HSA (Health Savings Account) - max contribution in 2023/2024 for singles is $3,850.
- ➢ Roth IRA - max contribution in 2023 for those under fifty years old is $6,500.

> ➤ 401k - max contribution in 2023 is $22,500 for those under fifty years old.
> ➤ Taxable brokerage account – you can invest unlimited amounts here. (High income-earners typically use this account when they have maxed out all other investment accounts).
> ➤ Make sure that you pick low-fee index funds and diversify your portfolio.
> ➤ Ensure that you turn on auto-invest dividends. I do this in Fidelity. I'm pretty sure you can do this with other brokerage firms.
> ➤ Ensure that you set up automatic investments. Set it and forget it!
> ➤ Reallocate/rebalance your portfolio. Typically check your investments once a year. This is done when you have a three-fund portfolio. Search on YouTube to see how to rebalance your investment portfolio.

Note: Target Age/Date index fund automatically rebalances as you get closer to your retirement year.

> ➤ Never sell—just buy, hold, and stay the course. Remember, we are long-term investors, not day traders.

Assumptions: You have a job, you have determined to invest at least ten percent of your salary, and you're ready to Max It Out! This is how I would personally handle each scenario, but remember that the journey is *yours*, so Max It Out based on your personal needs!

Scenario 1: You're a newbie. You have no savings, you don't have a Roth IRA, you have a job, and the job provides a 401k match but no HSA (Health Savings Account).

> ➤ Invest in the 401k up to the match.
> ➤ Put the remaining money in an emergency fund money market or in a high yielding savings account.

Scenario 2: You have three to nine months of emergency savings, you're contributing to your 401k up to employer match, your job doesn't offer an HSA, and you don't have a Roth IRA.

> ➤ Continue saving towards your emergency fund and 401k up to employer match.
> ➤ Begin investing in a Roth IRA. Start small if your salary hasn't increased. Remember I started with twenty-five dollars a month.

Scenario 3: You have six or more months of emergency savings. Your job offers an HSA and 401k. You make enough to max out your Roth IRA.

> ➤ Continue saving towards your emergency fund.
> ➤ Continue investing in your 401k up to employer match.
> ➤ Invest in your company's HSA and make sure you invest the money.
> ➤ Max out your Roth IRA contribution.

Scenario 4: You're doing everything in Scenario 3, your salary allows you to max out on all investments.

> ➤ Continue saving towards your emergency fund.
> ➤ Max out your 401k contributions.
> ➤ Max out your HSA contributions.
> ➤ Max out your Roth IRA. (Check the salary restrictions. You cannot contribute if you make more than the current year's maximum salary rule.)
> ➤ If, after all bills are paid, all is maxed out above and you still have money left over, open a taxable brokerage account and invest the leftover money there.

Scan the QR code to download the **"Fund Tracking Sheet" for FREE!**

Take control of your investments with *My Fund Tracking Sheet*, a simple yet powerful tool to manage and track all your investments in one place.

Join the Movement

Scan the QR code below to access the **Feminine Finance Mastery Community**—where ambitious women learn to invest with confidence, build wealth, and live in abundance.

Ready to Glow-Up Your Finances?

Hey Queen—if you've been loving these lessons, imagine the transformation you'll have inside my **Feminine Finance Mastery Community** 💎.

Inside, you'll get:

- ➢ Supportive sisterhood
- ➢ Step-by-step investing guidance
- ➢ Tools to grow your first $10K portfolio
- ➢ Challenges + activations that help you shift from scarcity to abundance
- ➢ Scan the QR code to join us now and start building your wealth the feminine way.

Recommended Books

This is the list of books I recommend:

Book	Author	Favorite Quote
The Automatic Millionaire	David Bach	"A latte spurned is a fortune earned."
The Simple Path to Wealth	JL Collins	"If your lifestyle matches—or god forbid exceeds—your income, you are no more than a gilded slave."
Rich Dad Poor Dad	Robert T. Kiyosaki	"The rich focus on their assets while everyone else focuses on their income."
The Four Pillars of Investing	William Bernstein	"If you find yourself stimulated in any way by your portfolio performance, then you are probably doing something very wrong. A superior portfolio strategy should be intrinsically boring."

Book	Author	Favorite Quote
The Millionaire Next Door	Cotter Smith	"One of the reasons that millionaires are economically successful is that they think differently."
Money Master the Game	Tony Robbins	"Take the money you save on fees and reinvest it for compounded growth. This strategy is another fast lane to freedom."
Unshake-able	Tony Robbins	"As Warren Buffett says, "Risk comes from not knowing what you're doing."

My Funds Tracking Spreadsheet

Broker	Account Type	Fund	Description	*GER	*NER	Amount	Date Checked	Comment
Vanguard	Index Fund	VTSAX	Vanguard Total Stock Market Index Fund	.04%	.04%	$95,000	01/01/23	Need to strategize

*GER – Gross Expense Ratio

*NER – Net Expense Ratio

401k Matching Examples

Some of my friends and clients don't understand how 401k matching works, so I thought including this example would be helpful. So how do I calculate 401k matching? I've included a visual representation below the examples.

What is the company matching? What is your salary?

Example 1: Company's match is $1 per dollar on the first 3% of pay.

- ➤ Calculate 3% of your pay. So, if you make $50,000 a year, 3% x 50,000 = $1,500
- ➤ $1,500 is the max the company will match per year.
- ➤ Because the company will give you $1 per every dollar you invest, you will need to invest $1,500 of your pay, and your company will give you $1,500. At the end of year one, you will have $3,000 invested plus interest (amount varies depending on your investment choices)

Example 2: Company's match is fifty cents per dollar on 6% of pay.

- ➤ Calculate 6% of your pay. Using the same salary, $50,000 a year, 6% x 50,000 = $3,000
- ➤ $3,000 is the max the company will match per year.

> In this case the company will give fifty cents per dollar unlike Example 1. Calculate $3,000 x 0.50 = $1,500 is your company's match.
> You will need to invest $3,000 of your pay and your company will give you $1,500. So at the end of the year, you will have $4,500 invested plus interest (amount varies depending on your investment choices)

Example 3: Company's match is $1 per dollar on the first 2% of pay and fifty cents per dollar on the next 4%. This one is a little tricky, but companies do this.

> Calculate 2% of your pay. Using the same salary, $50,000 a year, 2% x 50,000 = $1,000
> $1,000 is the max the company will match at $1 per dollar.
> Next, calculate the next 4% of your pay, 4% x 50,000 = $2,000
> You will need to invest $3,000 of your pay. Your company will give you $1,000 for your $1,000 contribution (first 2%), then give you $1,000 for the $2,000 contribution (next 4%).

Assuming you make a $50,000 annual salary:

Employer Match	Your Annual Contribution	Your Employer's Annual Contribution	Total
$1 per dollar on first 3% of pay	$1,500	$1,500	$3,000
$0.50 per dollar on 6% of pay	$3,000	$1,500	$4,500
$1 per dollar on first 2% of pay and $0.50 per dollar on the next 4% of pay	$3,000	$2,000	$5,000

Summary of Money and Life Lessons

Lesson #1: Save 10% for yourself, invest in a Roth IRA.

Lesson #2: Save $1,000 for emergencies.

Lesson #3: Set it and forget it!

Lesson #4: Don't stop learning.

Lesson #5: Boost contributions with each raise.

Lesson #6: Seek help without hesitation.

Lesson #7: Prioritize mental health!

Lesson #8: Turn setbacks into opportunities.

Lesson #9: Recognize your own value.

Lesson #10 Read for empowerment.

Lesson #11: Embrace the stock market, hold on.

Lesson #12: Negotiate your salary!

Lesson #13: Consolidate 401k accounts.

Lesson #14: Don't take ghosting personally.

Lesson #15: Snowball method for debt payoff.

Lesson #16: Stay humble.

Lesson #17: Speak up!

Lesson #18: Switch jobs for higher pay.

Lesson #19: Short sales require resilience.

Lesson #20: Monitor your investments.

ACKNOWLEDGEMENTS

First and foremost, I want to thank God for planting the seed for me to write this book. I thank our Creator for everything that he's done for me, for his protection, his love and compassion. He's made everything possible in my life.

I'm grateful for the many wonderful people I've met throughout my life. I'm a firm believer that people come to your life for a reason and for a season, maybe to teach you a lesson about what you don't want and perhaps to make that season one full of joy, laughter, and happiness. We must embrace both lessons.

I want to thank Mr. Andre Williams. Andre was my LPO (Leading Petty Officer) during my Navy days. You planted that seed to investigate a Roth IRA. I took the seed, planted it, watered it, and have seen it grow. Thank you for your guidance and mentorship and twenty-three years of camaraderie.

My daughter, Mia, is the drive and force that made me unstoppable at whatever personal and financial goal I've set. Many decisions I've made were in her best interest to make sure that I provide and protect her so she doesn't have to struggle as much as I did.

My mom, Delmi, for doing the best that she could, especially when women didn't have as many opportunities as we do today. I love you, Mom. Thank you for bringing that bread and cold chocolate milk so that when I opened my eyes, there you were with your sweet, caring voice. "Levantese," which is "Get up" in English, and you handed me those two delicious treats because my drunk uncles had eaten my dinner and I went to sleep with my stomach growling. This was a typical, everyday thing—if you're late coming home from playing with the neighborhood kids, you're not eating. Someone will get their hands on your food.

To my sisters, I love you girls. Thank you for looking up to me. Thank you for the emotional support and all the love that you always give me. You girls have come through for me during those days when I was working full-time and going to school full-time as well. You took care of my daughter when I needed you to step in to help me. Thanks. Remember, I do this for you guys, to serve as an example to you that possibilities are limitless.

Jeremy Schneider, thank you for taking my call and looking at my portfolio when you *just* started your IG page @personalfinanceclub. I DM-ed him and asked him to look at my portfolio, and he so kindly did. I was lucky because I don't think he does that anymore. Not many people will take the time out of their lives to help a stranger and you did! I learned so much from you along my journey, so I have to say, thank you!

Lastly, I want to thank Jeana and Lamont Bowling. Thank you for your wonderful friendship and inclusion. You guys always cheer and praise all those kids from Roosevelt who came from that hard-knock life and are now full-fledged adults. You motivated us and to this day, both of you are the epitome of grace and selflessness. Pure, genuine care for anyone and everyone who crosses your path. I am blessed that God put you in my path. I love you both!

ABOUT THE AUTHOR

Meet Brenda Carolina Paz, a dynamic author hailing from Somerset, New Jersey. Born in Honduras and raised in the U.S., Brenda's journey is a testament to unwavering determination. Juggling the roles of a single parent and a Navy veteran, she earned her MBA, embodying resilience, and hard work. Currently thriving as a full-time Senior Business Analyst in Financial Technology, Brenda's writing mirrors her diverse experiences. Her words not only reflect a profound personal journey but also serve as a beacon of inspiration. Through her unique perspective, Brenda passionately shares insights and lessons, enriching the world with her wisdom.